THIS BOOK BELONGS TO

_____

FROM

_____

I AM GRATEFUL FOR YOU BECAUSE

_____

_____

_____

_____

Gracie The Grateful Giraffe
by: Brianna Kuhl
Published By: Pink Papa's Publishing House

Books with a Purpose

www.BookswithAPurpose.com
www.PinkPapasPublishingHouse.com

ISBN-13: 979-8-9873551-8-3

THANK YOU
FOR SUPPORTING BILLY'S PLACE

Billy's Place provides a safe community of comfort and companionship to kids and families experiencing grief, no matter where they are on their journey, through support groups, remembrance events, and education. We help families rediscover moments of happiness without guilt. We nurture these moments as signs of hope for more promising days ahead.

www.billysplace.me

10% OF ALL BOOK SALES ARE DONATED TO BILLY'S PLACE! THANK YOU FOR CONTRIBUTING TO THEIR INCREDIBLE MISSION! SCAN THE CODE TO LEARN MORE!

DEDICATION

This book is dedicated to my incredible children, Bella and Carson (Doodle). The thing I am most grateful for in this life is that I get to be your Mom. I love you both more than you'll ever know.

ABOUT THE AUTHOR

 Brianna Kuhl is a wife, mother, and certified Life Coach. Brianna personally used the power of gratitude to transform her own life. Now she passionately teaches and practices it with her children every day.

Brianna believes the power of gratitude is one of the most important tools you can learn in life. Brianna wrote this book because she wants every child to be exposed to the power of gratitude and learn how to apply the practice in their own life.

Gracie

The Grateful Giraffe

By: Brianna Kuhl

Bella couldn't sleep. She was far too excited! Tomorrow her second-grade class was taking a trip to the zoo. Bella had never been on the school bus before. Her best friend, Zoey, said the bus had no seatbelts! She couldn't wait to see for herself.

Bella was even more excited to see the animals. Kansas City had one of the few zoos that kept koalas. They were Bella's favorite animals, but she'd only ever seen them in cartoons.

She tossed, turned and tried counting sheep. But Bella had koalas on the brain...

"Wake up!" shouted Mom. "You missed your alarm!"

Bella opened her eyes and sat up in surprise. She must have finally fallen asleep! To her horror, she had also overslept.

"Hurry," said Mom, "or you'll be late for your field trip."

"OH NO!" cried Bella, leaping out of bed.

Bella landed on something sharp. "OW!" she yelled, hopping around on one foot.

She glared at a little plastic brick on the floor. The Lego must have been left there by her little brother.

"I told Doodle *not* to play in my room!"

Bella wasn't only worried about being late. Now she was sore and annoyed too! She pulled on her new zebra-print dress which she'd saved for today's trip. Bella ran downstairs, threw some waffles in the toaster and went to get her shoes. But Bella's left shoe was nowhere to be found.

"How can one shoe disappear?" asked Bella.
"I put both shoes by the door last night."
Bella searched everywhere... even behind
the cushions on the couch!

"I don't understand," she moaned.
"What *else* could go wrong?"
Suddenly, an awful smell filled Bella's nose.

"My waffles!" yelled Bella, running into the kitchen.

Bella's breakfast was burnt black. But she didn't have time to toast any more.

"I'll be in the car!" shouted Mom.

Bella quickly poured a glass of orange juice. She grabbed her jacket and the first shoes she could find. Bella wriggled into her rubber rain boots and ran out of the house.

Bella's boots were new and a bit too big.
As she ran to Mom's car, she tripped!

SPLASH!

Bella's new zebra dress was covered in juice.
Now the pattern looked more like a tiger!

"Nothing *ever* goes right for me," said Bella.
"How could this day get any worse?"

Sadly for Bella, the day *did* get worse. As Mom turned into the school, Bella's heart sank. The yellow school bus was already driving away. She was too late!

"How will I find out about the seatbelts *now*?" she moaned.

"Ask Zoey at the zoo," said Mom. "Don't worry, I'll drive you."

Bella hopped out of the car and ran to the zoo entrance. But Zoey wasn't waiting there!

"We picked groups on the bus," said Mr. Carter, the teacher. "You're in Austin's group."

Bella couldn't believe her bad luck. Austin was the new girl! She didn't know her at all.

As her group explored the zoo, Bella walked by herself at the back. She was very disappointed. Most of the animals were asleep! Finally, Bella arrived at the koala cage. There was a big sign fixed to the bars.

Koala Exhibit CLOSED.

That was the last straw. Bella sat on a bench and began to cry.

"Why do bad things always happen to me?" she wailed. "I woke up late, hurt my foot and burned my waffles. I ruined my dress, missed the bus and now I missed the koalas too!"

Bella was furious. "WHAT ELSE IS GOING TO GO WRONG?"

"Be careful what you say, Bella," said a voice. "The universe is listening."

Bella whirled around. No one was there! Just a giraffe on the other side of the path. The animal's head and long neck were leaning over the fence. It was looking right at Bella!

"It was me that spoke," said the giraffe. "My name's Gracie. It means grateful."

Bella frowned. "I'm not grateful for *anything* today. Everything's gone wrong. You wouldn't understand."

The giraffe blinked her long lashes. "You get to live in a house, don't you? You have your own bed and a blanket too?"

"Um... sure," said Bella.

"You have toys to play with, food to eat, and you don't have to walk everywhere?"

"That's right," replied Bella.

Gracie smiled. "If you just focus on what's going wrong, you'll only get more negative things to be upset about. Instead, try giving thanks to the universe for what you have. I think you'll find *many* reasons to be grateful."

The giraffe munched a leaf from a nearby tree. "Every day when I wake up, I give thanks for three new things. Today I said thank you for this tasty food, and for Bryn the zookeeper who keeps me clean. I also said thanks for my mom. She always sticks her neck out for me."

Gracie finished her leafy meal. "It's much better to be positive, Bella. Focus on the good things. The universe will send you even *more* things to be grateful for."

It was time for the giraffe's midday nap. As Gracie galloped away, Bella thought about her advice. She didn't think it would work, but decided to try it anyway.

KOALA Exhibit
CLOSED

Bella looked around. No one in her group was watching, so Bella closed her eyes.

"Thank you for my family, universe," she whispered, "and for my dog. Thank you for my friends. And thank you for the cute koalas, even though I didn't meet one."

Having said what she was grateful for, Bella felt better. She walked back to her group, who were sitting in the picnic area.

"Are you ready for lunch?" asked Austin's mom, who was helping on the trip.

"You bet," said Bella, "I burnt my breakfast. I'm starving!"

During lunch, Bella talked to Austin for the first time. She was pretty funny!

"Why did the elephant's car break down?" asked Austin. "Because he filled his trunk with water!"

Even better, Austin shared her cookies with everyone in the group.

Thanks for the food and fun lunch, thought Bella. *And for my new friend.*

In the afternoon, most of the animals were awake. Bella saw alligators, elephants and zebras! She stayed away from the terrifying tigers, in case they were confused by her dress. Later, Bella's group walked past the koalas again. When she saw the sign, she was delighted!

Koala Exhibit OPEN.

Some koalas were climbing the trees and others were cuddled together. Bella felt warm and full of love. The fluffy creatures were even cuter than she imagined!

"Wow," whispered Bella. "Thank you universe, for letting me see koalas today!"

Suddenly, it started to sprinkle with rain. Some kids screamed, worried about getting their sneakers wet. But Bella was happy and grateful for her rain boots. She could jump in the puddles all she wanted! Though the sky had turned gray, Bella felt sunny inside.

What a great day, she thought. *I'm having so much fun!*

"We've seen all the animals now!" said Austin's mom.
"Let's head back to the bus and meet Mr. Carter."

Bella's heart leaped. She would finally get to ride the
bus, all the way home. Soon, she'd see for herself if
there were seatbelts or not. Bella was so excited!

But before she left, Bella wanted to see a certain giraffe. She walked to the fence and waved at Gracie. She lowered her head toward Bella and blinked her long lashes.

Bella smiled. "I got to meet so many animals, Gracie. It's been such an awesome day!"

The giraffe smiled back. "I'm pleased to hear it. Remember, look for the good in every situation. If you can't find it, create it. There's always *something* to be grateful for."

"That's right," said Bella, stroking Gracie's fuzzy face. "I'm really grateful I met you."

GRACIE THE GRATEFUL GIRAFFE
WANTS TO KNOW WHAT YOUR GRATEFUL FOR

Go to
www.BooksWithAPurpose.com
And download FREE coloring pages
Learn how to Draw a Giraffe and print out your own
gratitude sheets!
Once you color them, upload them and use the
#GracieTheGratefulGiraffe for a chance to have your art
featured on the website!

FILL OUT THE "I AM GRATEFUL FOR YOU BECAUSE"
AND SEND IT TO SOMEONE YOU KNOW TO HELP US
HAVE A GRATITUDE RIPPLE EFFECT ON THE WORLD!